Warm Mittens and Socks

Dozens of Playful Patterns and Skillful Stitches to Knit, Crochet, and Embroider

Eva Trotzig

Photography by Malin Nuhma

Translated by Ellen Hedström

Skyhorse Publishing

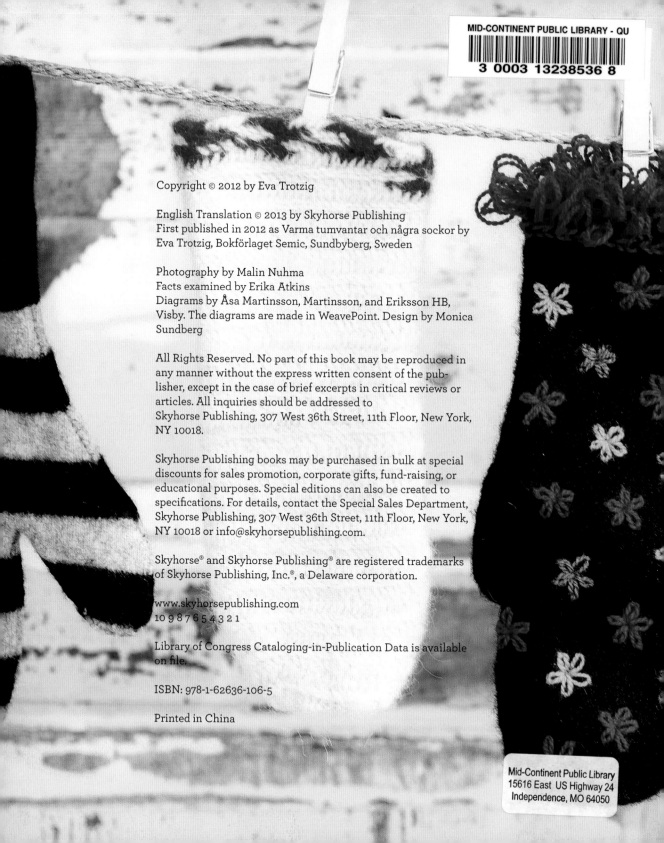

Copyright © 2012 by Eva Trotzig

English Translation © 2013 by Skyhorse Publishing
First published in 2012 as Varma tumvantar och några sockor by
Eva Trotzig, Bokförlaget Semic, Sundbyberg, Sweden

Photography by Malin Nuhma
Facts examined by Erika Atkins
Diagrams by Åsa Martinsson, Martinsson, and Eriksson HB,
Visby. The diagrams are made in WeavePoint. Design by Monica
Sundberg

Skyhorse Publishing books may be purchased in bulk at special
discounts for sales promotion, corporate gifts, fund-raising, or
educational purposes. Special editions can also be created to
specifications. For details, contact the Special Sales Department,
Skyhorse Publishing, 307 West 36th Street, 11th Floor, New York,
NY 10018 or info@skyhorsepublishing.com.

Skyhorse® and Skyhorse Publishing® are registered trademarks
of Skyhorse Publishing, Inc.®, a Delaware corporation.

www.skyhorsepublishing.com
10 9 8 7 6 5 4 3 2 1

Library of Congress Cataloging-in-Publication Data is available
on file.

ISBN: 978-1-62636-106-5

Printed in China

Contents

Introduction

Why are we still knitting by hand when the first knitting machine was built as early as the sixteenth century? The answer is simple: because it's fun. When we knit by hand we create something original; the results are never the same—even when two people knit according to the same pattern. Apart from the joy of knitting socks and mittens, it's a convenient project to take with you when you're "on the road," having a coffee, or watching television. A knitting project doesn't take up much room and you don't need very much material.

For this book, my friends and I knitted socks and mittens that mean something to us, and in doing so, I have been allowed to experience fantastic patterns that I would never have thought to create myself. We're driven to share the different ways of creating and knitting that we have learned throughout our lives and that we are passionate about.

Who are these friends then? Where do you find women—and men—who are prepared to share their patterns? Apart from myself, there were seventeen people who took part in this book and they all work with textiles. Some are amateurs and some are professionals, but they are united by the fact that they love to create. Here you will find knitted, crocheted, sewn, knotlessly knitted, and woven items, and of course, these socks and mittens and everything in between reflect our times and cultures, as well as the opportunities and limitations that surround us. A lot of love and care are woven into these warm clothes. Many of the mittens are made with yarn that has been crafted from Swedish wool and spun in Sweden, where I live and have my roots. Östergötlands Woolen Mill shows us that it is possible to produce beautiful and functional wool on a large scale, and at Herrviks and Grimslätts farms, the sheep lead a good life and quality yarns are produced on a smaller scale. These are perfect for knitting. As you can see, warm mittens can be locally produced—when it comes to knitting them, as well as when making the wool.

Handmade socks and mittens can also be a response to our need to reuse that which we already have. Worn out sweaters can be felted and sewn into mittens, and scraps of yarn can be used to make socks and mittens that are warm, felted, and functional.

This book is for those who know the basics of knitting and crocheting, but those who are not well versed in handicrafts can find good resources in a book shop or library. Many of the steps can also be learned on the Internet, and YouTube is a real goldmine.

I don't think it's too bold to state that you can find mittens for everyone here. These patterns all continue old traditions and create new ones. So be inspired to create using our ideas and your own. My hope in writing this book is that you will use the colors you and your friends love, play with the patterns, and have fun.

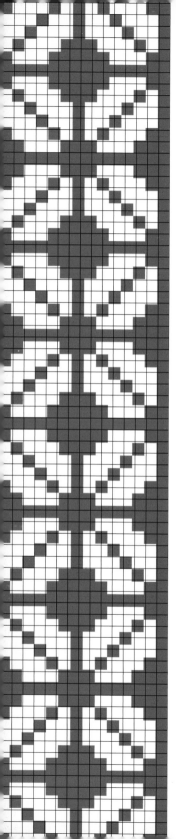

Traditions

Traditional mittens can be amazing creations. Mittens from the Baltic countries—often made with very thin knitting needles and several colors—can be works of art. The thin yarn, thin needles, and the skill of the knitter all result in something exquisite. Traditions live on and books with patterns are published. Even when it's hard to get hold of beautiful, thin yarn made from wool, patterns and styles live on with the help of synthetic yarns. These aren't able to give the same warmth, but the knowledge is kept alive. At the end of this book (page 92) is an excellent example of how a pair of fingerless mittens from Estonia have been re-created in Sweden.

Even in my country of Sweden, traditions are very much alive and are being passed on to new generations. In different regions of Sweden, different patterns and styles are kept alive. Gotland (an island off the coast of Sweden) has a treasure trove of mittens that are made with two colors. On Öland (another coastal island) they develop their own patterns, and in northern Sweden there are colorful mittens with yellow, red, and blue that are reminiscent of the Sami culture. Two-end knitting and Nalbinding (or knotless knitting) are traditions that we hope will always survive. Sometimes it happens that the same pattern appears in different places, and a mitten from Estonia and one from Sweden can have the same pattern without any connection.

Sweden doesn't only have its own traditions and creations. In today's society, handicrafts are enhanced by the fact that many Swedes have their roots in different countries and some of them come with their own traditions. In the world of weaving, I have seen women who came to Sweden as adults learn weaving techniques alongside other studies. Handicrafts create bonds between people, and the lack of a common language is not a hindrance. I personally had the fortune to meet many women through knitting many years ago, and it was a very giving experience, both craft-wise and socially.

Traditions are passed on in different ways. We like to have romantic notions about the old ways. By candlelight and maybe with a fire burning in the grate, an old grandma and a little girl sit by the hearth. The old teaches the young how to knit and a little ditty is repeated again and again, "insert the needle, bring the yarn over, slip the stitch off," and the little girl eventually learns. Maybe this is how it was taught before, but society has changed quite a bit since then. It's no longer the grandma who teaches knitting; it can just as easily be a father or even YouTube. Playfulness and ideas have no limits—one trend is graffiti knitting, whereby you cover bicycles and park benches in knit-work, or young people who knit covers for their cell phones and laptops. As you can see, we are constantly searching for new ideas for our work, and I hope this book can give both new ideas and established techniques. The search for the ultimate mitten or glove continues and maybe you will be the one to knit it.

Nalbinding mittens. The one on the left is felted.

Knitted Mittens

Herrviks Mittens

These mittens are really easy to make—the whole mitten is made in garter stitch. I made them for Kerstin M. of Herrviks Farm using yarn from her own sheep. She sells yarn in her little farm shop.

- **Size:** Ladies. If you use a thicker yarn and larger needles you can make men's mittens and smaller needles make children's mittens.
- **Yarn:** Herrviks 2-ply woolen yarn, approx. 1300–1600 yd/lb (2500–3000 m/kg)
- **Amount:** Around 1.75 oz (50 g)
- **Needles:** 2 (3 mm)
- **Gauge:** 10 stitches/2 inches (5 cm)
- **Skill level:** Easy

The last stitch in every row is twisted and the first stitch in every row is lifted as if making a knit stitch. All decreases and increases are made inside the edge stitch. Increase by knitting twice into the same stitch: first make one knit stitch and then one twisted stitch. Decrease by knitting two stitches together.

Remember, there is no rule stating that a pair of mittens need to be the exact mirror image of each other. They belong together for other reasons—the colors either match, or they don't.

Cast on 30 stitches. Change color on the side where you aren't decreasing. The yarns can be tied together; you don't need to attach the yarn if a row of rug knots will be sewn at the top edge. On the second row, increase by 1 stitch before the edge stitch, then increase every other row for a total of 3 times. Increasing and decreasing is done on even rows. Knit 2 rows. Then decrease a stitch every other row for a total of 3 times.

When you have decreased 3 times, knit two rows, and on the next row cast off 10 stitches. Immediately add 18 new stitches and knit a row. Now increase every other row until you have 47 stitches. Knit 6 rows, then reduce until you have 38 stitches. Increase again until you have 47 stitches and knit 6 rows, then reduce the stitches again.

When 43 stitches remain, cast off 20 stitches from the wrist and immediately add 10 new stitches. Increase and decrease for the top of the thumb as before. Continue to reduce on the finger side. When you have 30 stitches, cast off. Sew the mittens together and end by making a rug knot at the wrist by cutting yarn into 3 inch (8 cm) bits and using a few threads with a crotchet needle. Pull the yarn through and make a knot. Or pick up a stitch at a time on the top and knit a row in garter stitch.

Aftercare: Clean the mittens in warm soapy water. Rub them so that they felt slightly. You can form the mittens to make a thinner "cuff"—a washboard might help to do this. See page 107.

Knit the mittens with needle size 4 or 6 (3.5 mm or 4 mm) to make them loosely knitted. You can then felt them to the required size.

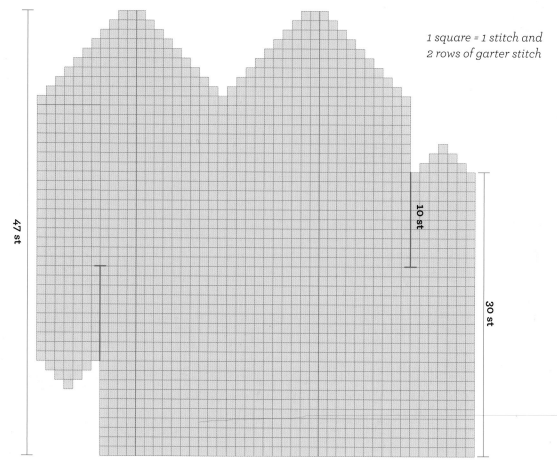

1 square = 1 stitch and
2 rows of garter stitch

47 st

10 st

30 st

This mitten can be made using remnants. If you change yarn at the wrist and make a rug knot, you don't need to attach the threads. If you're wondering how far a piece of yarn will get you, it's a good rule of thumb that you need about three times the length of the side that is being knitted.

Hulda's Stripy Mittens

Hulda Lundin (1847–1921) was at the forefront when it came to teaching handicrafts to girls. She founded a school for teachers and her methods have endured for decades. Her methods were built around the goals of creating easy, simple looking, and functional items. My friend Björn has recreated one of the patterns included in Hulda Lundin's classic book.

- **Size:** Children/ladies/men
- **Yarn:** Visjö from Östergötlands woolen mill, about 1600 yd/lb (3000 m/kg)
- **Amount:** About 3½ oz (100 g)
- **Needles:** Size 1 (2.5 mm). Two short circular needles, one long circular needle, or a set of double pointed needles
- **Skill level:** Easy

The whole mitten, except the cuff, is made in rib stitch.

Cast on 65, 69, or 73 stitches. When the stitches are divided among the needles, the first and last stitches are knitted together so that the number of stitches is reduced by one stitch. Björn has used a different way: he has knitted back and forth and left a space for the thumb in the middle of the mitten and then has carefully sewn the mitten together.

Do a rib knit, 2 knit, 2 purl for 4¾ inches (12 cm) if you want the mitten to have a cuff; if not, for 5½ inches (14 cm). 12 stitches are placed on a thread or a safety pin and 12 new stitches are cast on.

Knit until you get to the edge of the index finger where you begin to decrease. First round of decreasing: the purl stitches are knitted together, next round knit without decreasing, third round knit together over the purl stitch, round 4 knit in stockinette stitch. Then knit 2 stitches together until 6 or 8 stitches remain. The yarn is pulled through and secured.

The thumb is knitted by taking the stitches from the thread (or pin) and picking up 12 new stitches as well as 2 more on each side (a total of 28 stitches).

When the thumb is long enough you decrease in the same way as for the rest of the mitten, but the rows are knitted without the stockinette stitch in between.

If you want a cuff, pick up stitches from the first round and knit about 20 to 26 more rounds, either alternating between knit and purl or knitting 6 purl and 6 knit rounds until you reach the required length. Bind off and secure the threads.

Wash the mittens. The ribbed stitching may stretch when you wear the mittens; in this case, just dip them in water and gently reshape to make them just like new.

The mittens can be knitted using two needles and sewn together.

Thumb Sucking Mittens

A variation on Hulda's stripy mittens, these little baby mittens are perfect for an avid thumb sucker. Of course you should rinse and wring the mittens with a towel as often as you can so they are dry for the next trip in the stroller.

- **Size:** Baby
- **Yarn:** Visjö from Östergötlands woolen mill, about 1600 yd/lb (3000 m/kg)
- **Amount:** About 1 oz (25 g)
- **Needles:** 0 or 1 (2 or 2.5 mm). Two short circular needles, one long circular needle, or stocking needles
- **Skill level:** Easy

Cast on 40 stitches.
Knit in a round, 5 rows purl, 5 rows knit, and 5 rows purl, 1 row knit. Then you continue with the whole mitten in rib stitch, 2 knit, 2 purl. Knit 25 rows, place 10 stitches on a thread and on the next row cast on 10 new stitches. Knit 25 rows in rib stitch. Decrease at the fingertips by knitting 2 purl stitches together on a row. On the next row, knit the knit stitches together. Then knit them together 2 and 2 and pull a thread through the remaining ones.

The thumb: Take the stitches from the thread. Cast on 10 new stitches and knit 14 rows and then decrease in the same way as the mittens. If you don't want a hole for thumb sucking, pick up 10 stitches instead of casting on 10 new ones.

Hedvig's Knitted Mittens

Hedvig has interpreted these mittens for school in a most personal way. She got the pattern from Hulda Lundin's instructions, studied the picture, and then knitted freehand.

- **Size:** Preteen
- **Yarn:** 2-ply woolen yarn, around 1600 yd/lb (3000 m/kg)
- **Amount:** About 1.75 oz (50 g)
- **Needles:** Size 2 (3 mm) sock needles or a circular needle at least 24 inches (60 cm) long
- **Gauge:** 13 stitches/2 inches (5 cm)
- **Skill level:** Easy

Start by casting on 60 stitches. Knit in stockinette stitch. Improvise and experiment while you work. Do a few purl stitches and change the color now and again.

When you get to the thumbs, place 11 stitches on a needle or thread, and cast on 11 new ones. Continue knitting the round.

Decreasing at the fingertips: Divide the stitches and knit 2 together at 4 points on each round until 8 stitches remain. Thread the yarn through the stitches.

The thumb: Pick up 11 new stitches and take the 11 from the thread, knit until the thumb is the length you require and decrease by knitting 2 stitches together. Knit until you have 6 stitches left and pull the thread through the stitches.

Pick up 60 stitches at the top and knit in rib stitch, 2 knit and 2 purl. Bind off loosely so that the edge isn't pulled tight. Secure all the threads, soak the mittens, and lay them out to dry.

Be playful and let your fantasy run wild when you adorn your mittens. Pearls, pretty buttons, and embroidery can all be used. Don't be too practical or limit your imagination.

Children's Mittens with Little Men

Sick of nagging your kids to wear their mittens? Here's a way to make a mitten into a toy. It's both fun and practical.

- **Size:** 3–5 years
- **Yarn:** Visjö from Östergötlands woolen mill, 2-ply wool yarn, around 1600 yd/lb (3000 m/kg)
- **Amount:** About 1 oz (25 g) and some remnants
- **Needles:** Size 1 (2.5 mm). Two short circular needles, one long circular needle, or sock needles
- **Gauge:** 14 stitches/2 inches (5 cm)
- **Skill level:** Easy

Cast on 40 stitches. Knit in rib stitch, 2 knit, 2 purl, for 2½ inches (6 cm) and change to a stockinette stitch.

After about 2 inches (4.5 cm), place 8 stitches on a thread. On the next row, knit 7 stitches over the thread. Increase 1 stitch so that you have 40 stitches again.

After the thumb marker, knit 2.8 inches (7 cm).

Decrease 4 stitches evenly across the round.

Next round: Knit 4 stitches, knit 2 together.

Knit 4 rounds in stockinette stitch. Knit 3 stitches, then 2 together. Knit 3 rows in stockinette stitch, knit 2 stitches, then 2 together. Knit 1 row in stockinette stitch, then 2 together until 5 stitches remain.

The thumb: Take the stitches from the thread and make sure the thumb has 15 stitches. Knit using the main color for 1 inch (2.5 cm) and then use white yarn for ½ inch (1.5 cm).

Decreasing the thumb: Knit 2 stitches, then 2 together on the first round. Next row knit 1 stitch, then 2 together, and then 2 together until 5 stitches remain. Thread the yarn through the remaining stitches.

Secure all the threads and wash the mittens. Embroider the faces and place a tuft at the tip of the thumb.

Reflector Mittens

I got to know Eva when we were training to become professional weavers. Eva had been given a pattern that showed a clever way to create warm, soft mittens, from her second cousin Ulla. Eva's daughter Johanna designed the mitten decorations, which are made from reflective material. As Eva has an eye for color, she has made her mittens in colors that blend well together.

- **Size:** Ladies/men's
- **Yarn:** 3½ oz (100 g), 2-ply woolen yarn, plaid yarn, about 1600 yd/lb (3000 m/kg)
- **Amount:** 3½ oz (100 g)
- **Needles:** Size 7 or 8 (4.5 or 5 mm). Two short circular needles, one long circular needle, or a set of double pointed needles
- **Skill level:** Easy

Cast on 48/58 stitches.
Knit in stockinette stitch for about 8 inches (20 cm), about 52 rounds. Place 10 stitches on a thread for the thumb and cast on 10 new stitches.
Continue in stocking stitch for about 5 inches (12 cm) (32 rows).
Knit together every 4th stitch with the next one.
Knit 4 rows.
Knit together every 3rd stitch with the next one.
Knit 3 rows.
Knit together every 2nd stitch with the next one.
Knit 2 rows.

Knit the stitches together in twos to the end of the round and pull a thread through the remaining stitches.

The thumb: Pick up 10 stitches from the thread and pick up 12 new ones. Knit 18 rows in stockinette stitch. Knit the last two stitches together on each needle (if using 4 needles; if not, 4 stitches evenly distributed across the round).
Knit together at 4 points on each round until 4 stitches remain. Pull the thread through the rest of the stitches. Secure the threads.

Felting: Place in the washing machine—feel free to put them in with other clothes—at 104°F (40°C). Use only a small amount of detergent. Pull the mitten into the shape you want, then rub or brush the surface when the mittens have dried.
Read more about felting on pages 107–108.

Kerstin's Lost Mitten

It's easy to lose a pair of mittens—almost too easy. Usually we don't pay much attention to it but when we lose homemade mittens, we feel the loss a bit more deeply. A while back, Kerstin S. lost one of her mittens. She came to me and asked if I could make a new one for her from the same pattern and this was the result. We think this mitten with a wrist has its origin in the East—maybe Finland—but we don't know for sure. However, they are fun and easy to make.

- **Size:** Ladies
- **Yarn:** Saga from Järbo, 100% wool. About 1100 yd/lb (2080 m/kg)
- **Amount:** 2 skeins of the main color and remnants for the pattern
- **Needles:** Size 2 (3 mm). Two short circular needles, one long circular needle, or a set of double pointed needles
- **Gauge:** 16 stitches/2 inches (5 cm)
- **Skill level:** Average

Cast on 66 stitches, divide them evenly on the long circular needle or two circular needles with 33 stitches on each side, or on a set of double pointed needles with 17, 16, 17, and 16 stitches.

Knit 2 rounds in stockinette stitch and then a round of eyelet holes (2 stitches together, 1 stitch yarn over [YO] for the rest of the round). Then do 3 rounds stockinette stitch.

Border 1 (7 rounds). 2 rounds in stockinette stitch. Border 2 (8 rounds). 3 rounds in stockinette stitch. Border 3 (3 rounds). 3 rounds in stockinette stitch. One round of eyelet holes: 1 YO, 2 stitches together, 3 knit stitches. Repeat to the end of the round. On the next round bind off 12 stitches until you have 54 stitches. If you want the borders to finish evenly, decrease 2 stitches after the fourth border. (These stitches are cast on again after the fifth border.) 3 rounds stockinette stitch. Border 4 (7 rounds). 5 rounds stockinette stitch. Border 5 (3 rounds). Immediately after this border place 12 stitches on a thread for the thumb. On the thread that has been pulled through the stitches, knit new stitches and continue with the mittens (they make 11 stitches, so you need to increase by one stitch). Do 3 rounds in stockinette stitch. Border 6 (5 rounds). 3 rounds in stockinette stitch. 1 row of dots: 1 stitch using the pattern color, 2 stitches using the main color for the rest of the round. 1 round in stockinette stitch. Then repeat border 1 for 15 rounds.

Decreasing at the fingertips: The first 2 stitches on the top and bottom side are knitted together twisted and the last 2 are knitted together normally, giving the edge a nice finish. When 8 stitches remain, remove the yarn and thread through the stitches.

Place the thumb stitches on the needle, increase to 24 stitches, and knit 6 rounds in stockinette stitch and then follow the pattern according to the diagram on the top side and underside. After the pattern, knit 2 rounds in stockinette stitch and decrease for the tip of the thumb as you did for the fingertips. When 8 stitches remain, pull the thread off and through the stitches.

Sew a hem at the top edge so that the mittens get a nice scalloped edge. Plait, quick knit, or braid a band to thread through the eyelet holes. Add an extra tuft at the beginning and end of the band.

Wash the mittens and lay them out flat to dry. Don't lose them!

Rose Mittens

When the Baltic States were freed, I bought a pair of mittens from Latvia at a boutique in Stockholm. They were made from a rather rough woolen yarn and I didn't think they were particularly comfortable. However, one day it got really cold and I couldn't find any other mittens. When I sat on the bus wearing them, a woman suddenly said, "Don't you have a lovely pair of mittens." It then hit me that I could make a pair of these mittens in a softer yarn, which is exactly what I did.

- **Size:** Ladies, smaller/larger
- **Yarn:** 2-ply wool yarn, around 1350–1600 yd/lb (2500–3000 m/kg)
- **Amount:** Main color about 2½ oz (70 g) and remnants for the pattern
- **Needles:** Size 0 or 1 (2 or 2.5 mm). Two short circular needles, one long circular needle, or a set of double pointed needles
- **Gauge:** 16 stitches/2 inches (5 cm) with size 0 or 15 stitches/2 inches (5 cm) with size 1
- **Skill level:** Average

Cast on 64 stitches using one of the colors for the pattern. Knit one row in knit stitch. Change color and knit 2 rows in knit stitch. Divide the stitches between 4 needles or over one or two circular needles. Knit the rounds in stockinette stitch using the main color, but slip every 7th and 8th stitch for 5 rounds. Knit a round with all stitches—a slightly wavy edge is created when you slip a stitch for a few rounds. Follow the diagram. Knit a few easy borders. After 4 rows of roses place 16 stitches on a safety pin and cast on 14 new stitches. On the next round, increase by 2 stitches under the thumb space and then knit until a total of 8 rounds of roses have been made.

Bind off for the fingertips by decreasing in the sides of every row. Knit one stitch, knit 2 together twisted on one side and normal on the other.

The thumb: Take the 16 stitches from the pin and pick up 16 new ones, either knit a pattern or in the main color. Decrease as before.

Aftercare: Wash the mittens and shape them so they fit nicely around the wrist.

> The mittens can be knitted in different ways. The original mitten—and the way I usually knit it—has 3 colors on one of the rows of pattern. If you want to avoid that you can let the rose have a little bud. You can also make it easier by not making a pattern on the thumb.

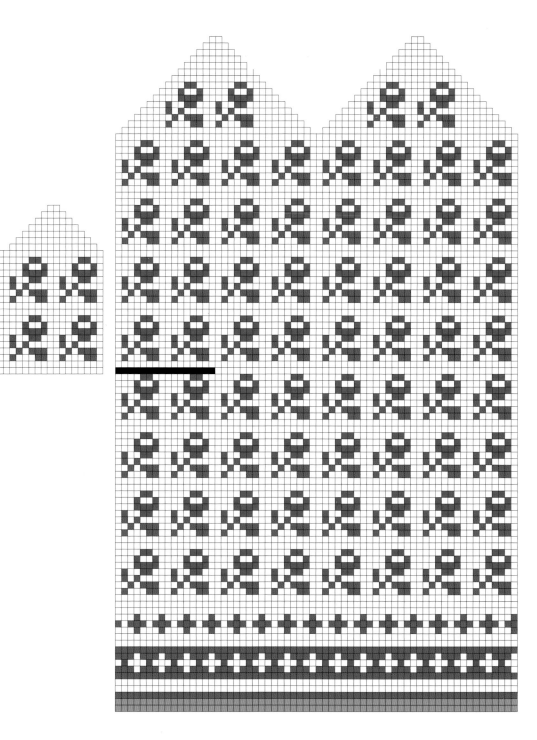

Girly Mittens

These mittens are the young girls' version of the Rose mittens.

- **Size:** 7–8 years
- **Yarn:** Visjö from Östergötlands woolen mill, about 1600 yd/lb (3000 m/kg)
- **Amount:** About 1.75 oz (50 g) of white plus remnants for the pattern
- **Needles:** Size 1 (2.5 mm). Two short circular needles, one long circular needle, or sock needles
- **Difficulty level:** Average

Cast on 48 stitches. Start by knitting a few rounds in color in garter stitch and then divide the stitches onto a circular needle or sock needles. Knit 5 rounds with white yarn, 1 purl, 1 knit. At the same time slip every 7th and 8th stitch in front of the white ribbed edging. After 5 rounds knit across all the stitches.

Make a few simple borders (each with 3 rounds) with a few rows of stockinette stitch in between and then carry on with the rose pattern.

After 3 rows of roses place 12 stitches on a thread and knit new stitches over the thread. (1 extra stitch needs to be cast on as you knit 11 stitches on the thread). After 3 rows of roses decrease for the fingertips by knitting the second and third stitch together on each side of the edge. (One side's decrease is done by knitting the stitches together twisted and the other side is knitted together normally.)

The thumb: This is knitted round with 24 stitches and is decreased on the underside of the thumb until you have 18 stitches. After 17 rounds you decrease at the top by knitting 2 stitches and 2 together until 6 stitches remain.

Remove the yarn and thread through the stitches.

Secure the thread and make sure that any holes at the sides of the thumb are closed.

Wash the mittens and lay them out to dry.

Get ready for a snowball fight.

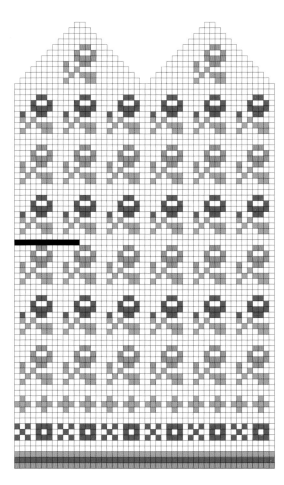

Herringbone Mittens

These mittens were made for thirteen-year-old David, but they will also fit a woman's hands. They are relatively easy to make and the pattern doesn't consist of any long floats.

- **Size:** Ladies, needle size 0; men's, needle size 1 (2 or 2.5 mm)
- **Yarn:** 2-ply woolen yarn with about 1600 yd/lb (3000 meter/kg) from Kampes spinning products
- **Amount:** Two hanks of 3½ oz (100 g) in two colors is enough for two pairs of mittens
- **Needles:** Size 0 or 1 (2 or 2.5 mm). Two short circular needles, one long circular needle, or a set of double pointed needles
- **Gauge:** 16 stitches/2 inches (5 cm) with needle size 0, 15 stitches/2 inches (5 cm) with needle size 1
- **Skill level:** Average

Cast on 66 stitches and divide them evenly across four needles or on a circular needle with 33 plus 33 stitches. Knit one row purl with a dark yarn, then change to a light yarn, knit 2 rows stockinette stitch and 2 rows purl. This prevents the edge from curling.

Follow the diagram where every square equals a stitch. Place the "edge stitches" first and last on the needles as it is hard to make the edge look pretty if the stitches are on different needles.

Knit straight along the edge until you reach the required length at the thumb grip. Place 15 stitches on a pin, the first 2 should be edge stitches. Cast on 15 new stitches. Knit the hand until the pinkie finger is covered and test it with your hand or against a drawing of the hand of the person who it's for. Decrease for the fingertips.

Decrease by knitting 2 stitches together on one side, on the other side knit 2 together twisted. These decreases are done with the edge stitches.

When 8 stitches remain pull a thread through them.

For the thumb, place the stitches from the pin onto the circular needle or the short needles. Knit following the pattern until you cover the thumbnail.

Decrease as you did for the fingertips.

Secure the threads. Wash the mittens, lay them out to dry, and shape them so they fit nicely around the wrist.

Herringbone Mittens

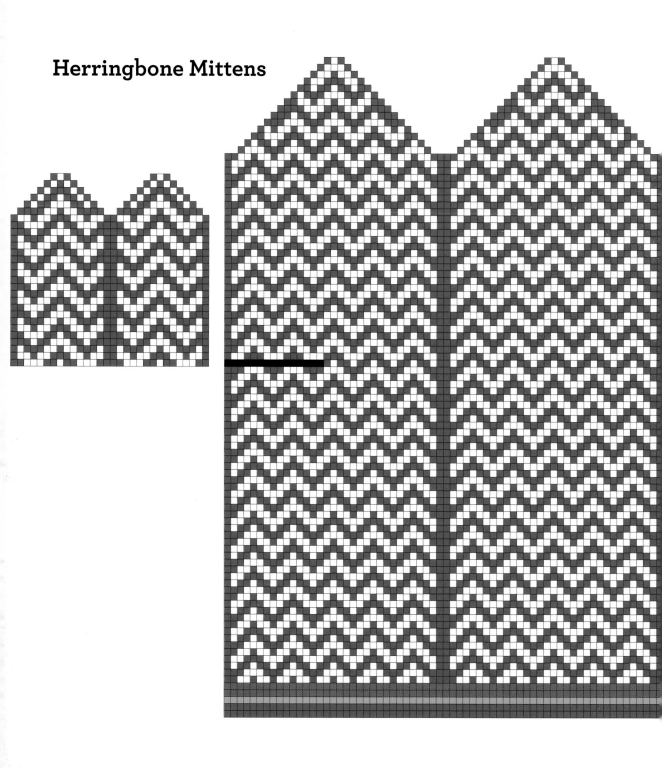

Erika's Grimslätt Mittens

Erika is a trained consultant in handicrafts and she does a lot of knitting. She made this pattern with the Norwegian county Bohuslän as her inspiration. The mittens are knitted in the natural colors of the yarn, with some streaks of blue (the sea) and fire engine red (the granite cliffs and sunset). Erika dyed the blue and fire engine red yarn herself.

- **Size:** Ladies
- **Yarn:** 2-ply woolen yarn 6/2 from Grimslätt Farm, around 1600yd/lb (3000 m/kg)
- **Amount:** 1.75 oz (50 g) light gray, 1.75 oz (50 g) dark gray, 0.35 oz (10 g) orange, and 0.35 oz (10 g) blue
- **Needles:** Size 4 (3.5 mm) or the size needed to get the right gauge. Two short circular needles, one long circular needle, or a set of double pointed needles
- **Gauge:** 24 stitches gives 4 inches (10 cm) in stockinette stitch
- **Skill level:** Average

The mittens are knitted in rounds. The pattern is made with two gray colors. The yarn that isn't being used in the pattern should run loosely on the wrong side of the knitting.

Some parts of the pattern show you how to knit using a set of double pointed needles so those using circular needles will need to adjust this.

Increase 1 stitch by lifting the yarn between 2 stitches and placing it on the left needle, then knitting the thread in purl.

Double ssk: slip 2 stitches as if you were making a knit stitch, knit the next stitch (the first on the next needle) using dark gray yarn, then pull the two slipped stitches over the knitted one = a 2 stitch decrease on the side of the mitten.

Cast on 42 stitches with orange yarn divided on four needles: 11/10/11/10 stitches or on a circular needle with 21 stitches on each side. Knit 4 rounds in knit stitch.

Knit one round in purl and at the same time increase 1 stitch at the beginning and end of each needle. 50 stitches are now divided on 4 needles: 13/12/13/12 stitches.

Take the orange yarn and knit according to the pattern.

On row 32 place 9 stitches on a thread for the thumbhole, see the marking for the right and left mitten on the diagram. Cast on 9 new stitches behind and knit them according to the pattern.

On round 55 start decreasing for the top of the mitten; slip the first stitch (it will be used in the double decrease at the end of the round), knit 22 stitches, end the round with a double ssk. Continue to decrease on every side of the mitten according to the diagram on each round until you reach round 62. After the last round of decreasing you should have 18 stitches left on the round. Place 9 stitches from each side of the mitten on two needles. Sew the stitches together using dark gray yarn and using mattress stitch.

The thumb: Place the 9 stitches from the thread on a needle. Pick up 11 stitches from the edge where you cast on the stitches in the thumb hole, see round 1 on the thumb pattern. Divide the 20 stitches for the thumb over 3 needles and knit round according to pattern for the thumb. The 3 rounds of decreasing are knitted with double ssk on the sides just as with the mitten.

Assembly: Fold in the orange edge and sew into the mitten in the purl round. Hem the edge—don't make it too taut.

Secure all the threads and wash the mittens in lukewarm water.

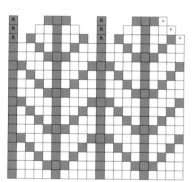

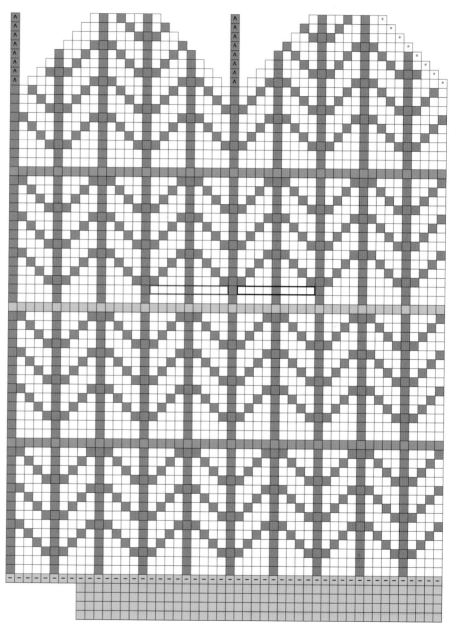

* slip first stitch on the
  round
^ double ssk
- purl stitch

Elsa's Mittens

My childhood was heavily influenced by our housekeeper Elsa. She was the one who patiently taught me how to knit and crochet. All the children wore her knitted socks, stockings, and mittens; it wasn't until I was twelve that I got a pair of store-bought socks. Elsa's mother knitted the most beautiful mittens I had ever seen. We called her "Auntie Granny" and she knitted mittens with a star pattern. Elsa was also gifted in making these, but there was something extra special about Auntie Granny's mittens. I want to honor my dear Elsa by including a description of a pair of children's mittens with a star pattern.

- **Size:** 4–6 years
- **Yarn:** Visjö from Östergötlands woolen mill, about 1600 yd/lb (3000m/kg)
- **Amount:** 1 oz (30 g) of each color
- **Needles:** Two short circular needles, one long circular needle, or a set of double pointed needles in size 1 (2.5 mm)
- **Gauge:** 17 stitches/2 inches (5 cm)
- **Skill level:** Difficult

Cast on 48 stitches and knit back and forth. 1 round garter stitch with the pattern color and 1 round purl with the main color, then 1 round purl stitch with the pattern color and 1 round garter stitch with the main color. This makes an edge that doesn't curl. Divide the stitches over 4 needles or on one or two circular needles.
Follow the pattern.
The thumb is placed on the back of the hand inside the 3 edge stitches. Take 9 stitches and place them on a separate needle. Cast on 9 new stitches; you will go back and knit the thumb at the end.
Decrease for the fingertips by knitting together the outermost edge stitches with the adjacent stitch. On the right side, the stitches are knitted together twisted; on the left, they are knitted together normally. When 8 stitches remain, pull the thread through them.

The thumb: Pick up one new stitch on each edge and decrease on the first round until you have 18 stitches. Make the thumb with the diagonal pattern. Knit the round on 18 stitches for 17 rounds (or according to your measurements). Knit the stitches together in twos until 6 stitches remain and pull the thread through.
Secure the threads and wash the mittens.
The mittens are knitted with the colors mirror imaged so you can tell the difference between left and right.

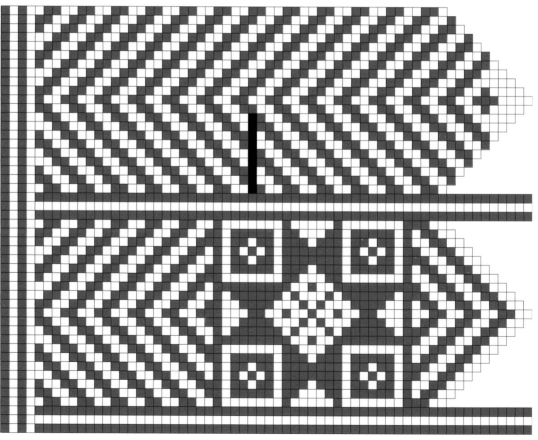

Bird Mittens

These mittens are a reworking of a Norwegian mitten from the 1950s. The pattern on the front has several rounds that are knitted in different ways but the inside of the hand has a simpler pattern.

- **Size:** Ladies
- **Yarn:** Visjö from Östergötlands woolen mill, about 1600 yd/lb (3000 m/kg)
- **Amount:** 1.75 oz (50 g) of each color and some in a contrasting color
- **Needles:** Two short circular needles, one long circular needle, or a set of double pointed needles size 0 or 1 (2 or 2.5 mm), (with size 1 the mittens are a size larger)
- **Gauge:** 17 stitches/2 inches (5 cm) with needle size 0 and 19 stitches/2 inches (5 cm) with needle size 1
- **Skill level:** Difficult

Cast on 68 stitches.

Cast on with a white and red thread, the white yarn creates the stitches and the red makes the edge. Knit one purl round with the white yarn and one knit and one purl round with the red. Divide the stitches into front and back. Follow the diagram.

For the thumb, place 13 stitches on a thread and cast on 13 new ones. Please note that the decrease starts earlier on the inside of the mitten as compared to the front.

Secure all the threads and wash the mittens.

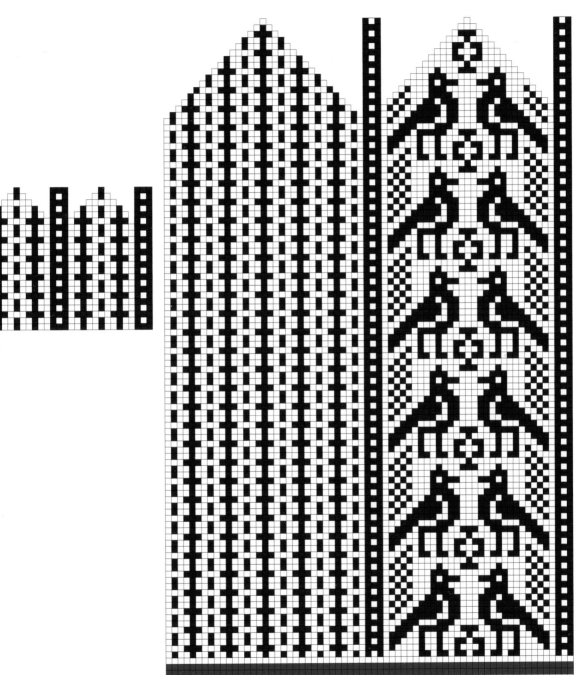

Inger's Mittens

Inger once visited our weaving circle, where, like days gone by, a group of men and women sit together to weave in company. She showed us a pair of beautiful woolen mittens her mother had bought at a thrift store in Orsa. The yarn was coarse, and as the mittens had not been washed or used we thought all the more reason to reknit them. What we have done here is knitted these same mittens after the same pattern, but we used another yarn and different needles.

- **Size:** Ladies/men's
- **Yarn:** Plaid yarn about 1600 yd/lb (3000 m/kg) from Järbo
- **Amount:** 1.75 oz (50 g) of each of the colors and some in a contrasting color
- **Needles:** Size 0 for ladies or 1 for men's. Two short circular needles, one long circular needle, or a set of double pointed needles
- **Gauge:** 17–19 stitches/2 inches (5 cm)
- **Skill level:** Average

Cast on 68 stitches. Make a decorative edge. The colors are twisted/twined on the front of the knitting and, depending on which direction you twist/twine the yarn, the pattern on the edges will vary.

Knit 7 rows with 2 stitches in the main color and 2 in the pattern color. When the border is finished, increase to 70 stitches. Follow the pattern.

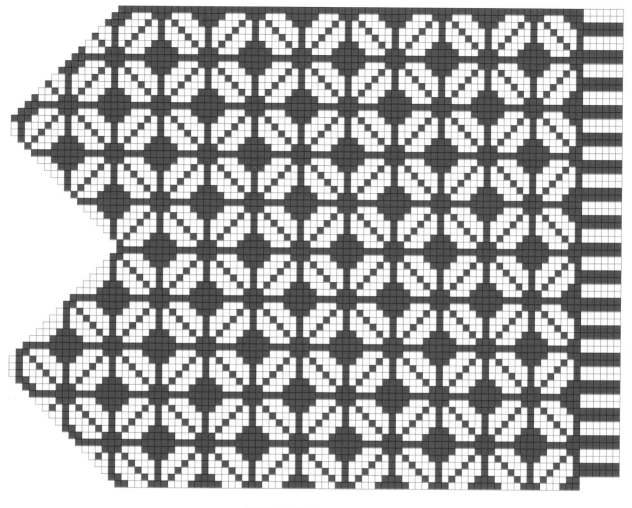

Found Mitten

This past winter, Margareta found a mitten in the snow. Since it was just after Christmas she figured that it must be a much missed Christmas present. She placed it in a spot where it could easily be found by the owner, and it disappeared. But when the snow melted she found just where she left it. This time Margareta took it home and made an exact copy.

The mittens, both the found one and the reconstructed one, are made using 2-ply woolen yarn.

Two-end or twined knitting keeps our heritage alive, in the same way that Nalbinding (knotless knitting) does. Using two threads that twine around each other gives a dense, strong mitten or sock, and if you would like to learn how to knit in this way we recommend the book Twined Knitting: A Swedish Folkcraft Technique by Birgitta Dandanell and Ulla Danielsson. Also, searching "twined knitting" on YouTube can net many good instructional videos.

Margareta would love for her found mitten to find its way back to its owner so the pair can be reunited!

Fingerless Mittens

Annika's Kimono Cell Phone Mittens

Annika sews, knits, and crochets. As her mom comes from Japan, Annika has drawn inspiration from traditional Japanese weaves. She made these mittens modern and chic by using bright colors and a model that was adapted for cell phone users (or knitters!).

- **Size:** Adult
- **Yarn:** Drops Alpaca 196 yd/1.75 oz (180m/50 g)
- **Amount:** 1 skein Drops Alpaca color 2928 (turquoise), 1 skein Drops Alpaca color 2921 (pink)
- **Needles:** Two short circular needles, one long circular needle, or sock needles size 2
- **Gauge:** 12 stitches/2 inches (5 cm), thicker when you are using two colors
- **Skill level:** Average

Cast on 48 stitches on the sock needles with the pink yarn doubled (knit in a round). The whole mitten is knitted with the yarn doubled up.

Round 1–7: 2 knit, 2 purl, repeat to the end of the round to make the ribbing.

Round 8–9: Begin stockinette stitch (knit stitches).

Round 10–30: Knit according to the pattern (knit stitches), read the pattern from left to right, row by row. Keep the yarn tight when knitting with two colors to give the mitten a good shape.

Round 31–33: Knit stitch in pink yarn only.

Round 34: Weave in a loose thread in a contrasting color according to the thumb markings in the pattern. (Please note that the thumbs are placed differently on the right and left hand.) Place these 10 stitches on the needle again and knit them again using the main color.

Round 35–46: Knit stitch.

Round 47–53: 2 knit, 2 purl, repeat to the end of the round to make the ribbing.

The thumb: Pull out the thread marking the thumb stitches, pick them up on the needles, and pick up 2 extra stitches on the sides to avoid holes.

Round 1: Knit stitch using turquoise yarn.

Round 2: Knit stitch. Reduce 1 stitch over the 2 extra stitches that were picked up at the edges (=20 stitches).

Round 3–6: Knit stitch.

Round 7: Knit stitch. Knit 5 stitches, knit 2 together, repeat to the end of the round (=16 stitches).

Round 8–14: 2 knit, 2 purl to the end of the round.

Bind off and secure the threads.

Accordion Mittens

Warm and cozy, and when you're not wearing them they look like little periscopes! The fingerless mittens in this picture are knitted with a light gray plaid yarn in the purl stripes and a darker yarn (which was a remnant) in the knit stripes.

- **Size:** Smaller/larger
- **Yarn:** Järbos 2-ply plaid yarn, about 1600 yd/lb (3000 m/kg) for the purl stitch, yarn remnants for the knit stitch
- **Amount:** 1.75 oz (50 g) of the main color is enough for two pairs
- **Needles:** Size 1 for smaller or 2 for larger (2.5 or 3 mm). Two short circular needles, one long circular needle, or sock needles
- **Gauge:** 16–18 stitches/2 inches (5 cm)
- **Skill level:** Average

Cast on 40 stitches and knit in a round, five rounds purl stitch in light gray, 4 rounds in stockinette stitch in your color of choice, then one round garter stitch in light gray. Repeat these 2 color sections 9 times, on the last of the rounds of garter stitch in color, place the 8 stitches opposite those where you change color on a pin or thread, and on the next round (light gray garter stitch) cast on 8 new stitches. Knit a further light gray stripe, one color stripe, and end with a light gray stripe and bind off. Take the stitches from the pin and pick up a further 8 stitches in the thumb hole. Knit 5 rounds in purl stitch with light gray yarn, bind off.

Secure the threads and wash the fingerless mittens.

You can make these fingerless mittens on two needles and sew them together. However, the thumb has to be knitted in a round (or you can simply leave the thumb hole unframed).

Tutti Frutti Mittens

These fingerless mittens are very easy to make. Be careful to check how many rows you need to ensure that the mittens fit properly. The mitten is knitted back and forth in garter stitch.

- **Size:** Ladies, smaller/larger
- **Yarn:** Visjö from Östergötlands woolen mill, about 1600 yd/lb (3000 m/kg) in the main color and remnants in several different colors for the stripes
- **Needles:** Size 1 for the smaller size or 2 for the larger (2.5 or 3 mm)
- **Amount:** 1.75 oz (50 g) of the main color is enough for two pairs
- **Gauge:** 16–18 stitches/2 inches (5 cm)
- **Skill level:** Easy

Cast on 33 stitches. Knit in garter stitch. The mittens in the photo have 4 rows in the main color and 2 rows in a contrasting color throughout. The color change takes place at the top edge. The first stripe in the main color is knitted for 3 rows. After 8 stripes of color, knit a thumb hole on the second row in the main color.

Thumb hole: Knit 10 stitches, turn, slip 1 stitch, knit 2 stitches, turn, knit 3 stitches, slip the first one, and turn. Continue until the hole has 10 stitches. Continue knitting 9 stitches, 8 stitches, and so on until you have 2 stitches. Knit in this fashion to the end of the round on the mitten's top edge. Knit back and forth until you have 8 colored stripes. On the next stripe in the main color knit 3 rows. Bind off.
Top edge and bottom edge: pick up a stitch in every "groove" and knit 3 rows on the lower edge, and 5 rows on the top edge. Bind off.
Sew the mittens together, secure the threads, and wash them.

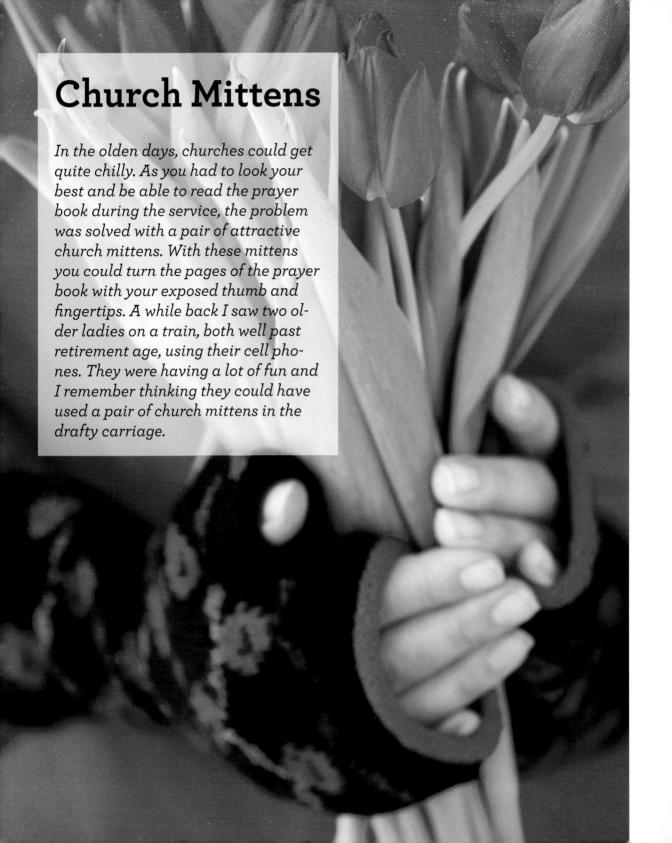

Church Mittens

In the olden days, churches could get quite chilly. As you had to look your best and be able to read the prayer book during the service, the problem was solved with a pair of attractive church mittens. With these mittens you could turn the pages of the prayer book with your exposed thumb and fingertips. A while back I saw two older ladies on a train, both well past retirement age, using their cell phones. They were having a lot of fun and I remember thinking they could have used a pair of church mittens in the drafty carriage.

Margareta uses this traditional pattern from Gotland with roses and shapes the mittens in an original way.

- **Size:** Ladies
- **Yarn:** Woolen yarn with about 1600 yd/lb (3000 m/kg), black, red, and green in two shades
- **Amount:** 2½ oz (70 g) black yarn and remnants in red and two shades of green
- **Needles:** Size 2, 1, and 0 (3, 2.5 mm, 2 mm, 1.5 mm)
- **Gauge:** Varies
- **Skill level:** Difficult

The mittens have the same number of stitches throughout (except by the thumb). The shape is achieved by changing needle size from 2 to 1 and then 0. Change them to keep a nice shape that follows the hand. The mittens are knitted in a round. Cast on 42 stitches and knit according to the pattern. First knit 4 rounds in purl with the red yarn, then 3 rows stockinette stitch with the main color—we have used black—then 3 rows purl with the main color, then 5 rounds stockinette stitch in the main color. Follow the pattern. When you are knitting 3 rows of roses, increase for the thumb. The thumb is placed on the side of the mitten under a rose. The starting point is marked with a line on the pattern. Increase on each side with 2 stitches. Continue with the rose pattern. Increase a total of 13 times spread over 15 rounds (increase every round 10 times and then twice every second round). Place the 28 stitches on a thread or pin and cast on 2 new ones to get the same number of stitches as you had before the thumb.

After the thumb, knit a row of roses and a row of leaves, 2 rounds in stockinette stitch with the main color, 2 rounds in purl with the main color, 4 rows in stockinette stitch with the main color, and finish with 6 purl rounds in red. Cast off.

Thumb: Take the 28 stitches and pick up 2 more. Knit in a round, making a row of green leaves and a red rose in the middle of the thumb. Finish off with 3 rounds in purl stitch and bind off.

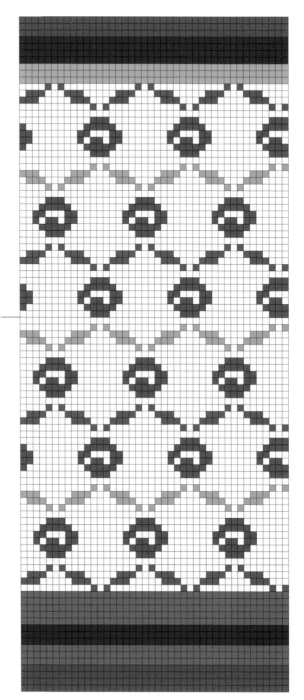

Crocheted Mittens

Hedvig's Crocheted Mittens

Anyone can crochet and knit. Thirteen-year-old Hedvig is an avid creator of amigurumi. (Amigurumi is the art of crocheting small, crazy figures of Japanese origin.) She made these simple mittens, doubling the yarn to make them extra warm and comfy.

- **Size:** Adult
- **Yarn:** Klippans 2-ply woolen yarn, about 1600 yd/lb (3000 m/kg), in two colors
- **Crochet hook:** 5/F
- **Amount:** About 3½ oz (100 g) of the main color (color 2), remnants for the rest (color 1)
- **Skill level:** Easy

Color 1 is used for the first 2 rounds and the last 2 rounds, color 2 is used for the rest.

Cast on 42 chain stitches doubling the yarn and using color 1.

Crochet single crochets into every chain stitch. Cut the yarn 6 inches (15 cm) from the last single crochet and make into a "ring," securing the thread neatly and change to color 2. Continue crocheting into the rear loop using single crochets and color 2 until the mitten measures about 4 inches (10 cm). Make a hole for the thumb.

Crochet 8 chain stitches. Skip 8 single crochets, as this is the space for the thumb. Continue to make single crochets from the 9th stitch (after the skipped stitches) for the remainder of the round. Then crochet single crochets into the chain stitches (8 stitches). You have now created a hole where you will crochet the thumb. Continue to make single crochets for another 5½ inches (14 cm) making the mitten 10 inches (24 cm) when it's time for the last rounds.

Finishing off: Round 1: Bind off 4 stitches, distributed evenly. You bind off 1 stitch by skipping a stitch.

Round 2: Crochet one round without binding off.

Every second round is crocheted as round 1 and every second as round 2.

After 8 rounds: Cut the yarn 6 inches (15 cm) from the single crochet, change to color 1 and crochet as round 2. Round 9 is the last round and is the same as round 2. Cut the yarn as before (6 inches [15 cm]).

Remember you need both a right and a left mitten. Secure all the threads.

Thumb: Crochet single crochets with color 2 in all the stitches in the thumb hole (16 stitches in total). Crochet single crochets until the thumb measures 2 inches (5 cm).

Tip of the thumb: Round 1: Decrease 4 stitches evenly spaced.

Round 2: Crochet a row without binding off.

Round 3: Same as round 1.

Round 4: Same as round 1 and this is the last round. Cut the yarn and sew together the tip of the thumb.

Sew together the straight top edge of the mitten so that the thumb hole is at the right spot for the mittens.

Crocheted Owl Mittens

*Mittens are an obvious children's accessory, so why not make them fun?
Annika crocheted mittens that look like owls for her daughter. They're both
adorable and practical.*

- **Hook:** 2/C
- **Yarn:** Marks and Kattens Eco baby wool color around 1 oz (25 g) = around 91 yards (83 m)

Crochet 32 chain stitches and make a closed ring.
Round 1: 33 double crochets in the chain stitch ring.
Round 2–5: 33 double crochets.
Round 6: Double crochets, decrease every 5th double crochet, finish with 3 double crochets (=27 double crochets).
Round 7–12: Single crochets.
Round 13: Thumb round.

Left hand
6 chain stitches, single crochet in the 6th stitch from the beginning of the round, single crochet to the end of the round
Round 14–30: Single crochets.
Round 31: 31 single crochets, finish off with a slip stitch (4 single crochets are added to compensate for the work twisting, increases: 2 single crochets in the same stitch, every 6th single crochet), cut and secure the thread.
Round 32–34: Change color: Crochet 14 stitches (on the thumb side of the mitten), turn.
Round 35: Crochet stitches 1 & 2 together, single crochet, crochet the last two stitches together (=12 stitches).
Round 36–39: Crochet together stitches 1 & 2, single crochet, crochet together the last 2 stitches.
Round 40: 4 single crochets, cut and secure the thread.
Round 41: Change color: 4 single crochets.
Round 42: Single crochets: crochet the first and last stitches together (=2 stitches).
Round 43: Single crochet: crochet the first and last stitches together, cut and secure.
Sew the opening for the fingers together and fold over the triangle toward the top side of the mitten (=not the thumb side) and secure.
Round 13: Thumb round.

Right hand
8 single crochets, 6 chain stitches, single crochet in the 6th stitch from the last single crochet, single crochet to the end of the round
Round 14–30: Single crochets.

Round 31: 36 single crochets, finish off with a slip stitch (4 single crochets are added to compensate for the work twisting, increase: 2 single crochets in the same stitch every 6th single crochets.
Round 32–34: Change color: Crochet 14 stitches (Note! Make sure this is on the mitten's thumb side and that the thumb is in correct position in relation to the left mitten), turn.
Round 35: Crochet together the first & second stitches, single crochet, crochet together the last two stitches (=12 stitches).
Round 36–39: Crochet together the first & second stitches, single crochet, crochet together the last two stitches.
Round 40: 4 single stitches, cut and secure the thread.
Round 41: Change color: 4 single crochets.
Round 42: Single crochet: crochet together the first and last stitches (=2 stitches).
Round 43: Single crochet: crochet together the stitches, cut and secure the thread.

Thumb: Round 1: 14 single crochets in the space for the thumb.
Round 2–10: Single crochets.
Round 11: Decrease. Crochet the stitches together in twos until you have 4 stitches remaining, cut the yarn and pull through the last stitches, secure.

Eyes: Crochet 3 chain stitches, make a closed ring with a slip stitch, crochet 1 single crochet in the same stitch, then 2 single crochets in every stitch 3 times, 1 slip stitch, cut the thread 8 inches (20 cm) from the hook, secure and sew the white of the eye onto the mitten. Make the iris on the white background using embroidery once you have attached the eye.

Embroidered Mittens

My sister-in-law Mona has sewn and embroidered many mittens throughout her life, and I've included some of them here. The light colored mittens were inspired by the ceiling in Väversunda church. She always sews a phone number into the mittens for those who have a tendency to lose them.

These mittens are made from Wadmal fabric. For this style it is important to choose a material that is felted, as the edges of the mittens do not get hemmed. Follow the pattern on page 66.

The components of the mittens are made simply by doubling up the material and sewing together along the edges. Embroider on the top half of the mitten and then sew the respective parts together in twos with a sewing machine. When finished, they need to be thoroughly pressed.

Mariana's Mittens

Mariana teaches weaving, so naturally her mittens are woven. However, in her own unique style, she's given the mittens a twist with the addition of embroidered flowers.

- **Warp:** Tuna yarn 6/2, about 1600 yd/lb (3000 m/kg)
- **Weft:** Same as the warp
- **Reed:** 40/10, one thread in the heddle and one in the dent
- **Width in reed:** 0.44 yards (40 cm)
- **Thread count:** 160 threads
- **Weave length:** 1.53 (1.40 m)
- **Tie on and thrums:** 0.6 yards (0.55 m)
- **Warp length:** 2.13 yards (1.95 m)
- **Skill level:** Easy

Weave in plain weave (tabby) with four wefts/½ inch (cm).

Cut down and zigzag the ragged edges.

Soak the fabric in lukewarm water for roughly an hour.

Felt in the washing machine on an 86°F (30°C) color cycle. If the fabric has not felted to the level you require, run it through the machine again in the same way.

The felting needs to be good enough that it's not apparent that the fabric is woven, but it still needs to be soft and smooth. As all washing machines are different, you should first do a test wash using a smaller bit of fabric (preferably together with other items, as it is the mechanical process that felts the fabric).

The pattern template

Place your hand on a piece of paper, keeping your fingers together but your thumb slightly protruding. Trace around it, leaving a ¼ inch (0.5 cm) margin outside the hand. Cut out the pattern.

Cut out four parts of the woolen fabric and, if you wish, the piece that makes the bottom part can be made slightly smaller than the top part. Place the parts against each other and sew together using small, closely spaced stitches and doubling the thread.

Turn the mitten the right way around and if you like, embroider the topside. Do the same with the other mitten, but make sure you get a right and a left mitten. Press the seams.

> When Mariana had tested different patterns for her mittens she got a taste for it and carried on, buying a pearl embossed sweater and a stripy tank top at a secondhand store. She felted these and made mittens from them. Here she has utilized both the stripes and the decorations. The ribbed edge of the tank top made the ribbing on the cuff and the edge of the red sweater made the edge of the mitten. When a worn, knitted item seems beyond all repair, you can at least make a pair of lovely mittens from it. Now that's recycling!

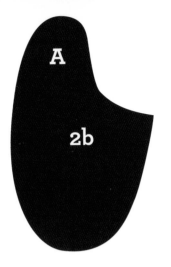

14 cm

14 cm

Sickan's Mittens

Here's a pair of warm mittens in boucle weave made by my weaving teacher, Kerstin L. She named the mittens after her little dog, Sickan. These are made in the same pattern as Mona's mittens on page 63 but here the fabric is the main feature and the boucle makes the mittens particularly warm.

- **Warp:** Borgs felted wool, 1600 yd/lb (3000 m/kg)
- **Weft:** Borgs felted wool and double knit (DK) merino superwash, around 1900 yd/lb (3500 m/kg) for the boucle
- **Reed:** 50/10 one thread in the heddle and one in the dent
- **Width in reed:** 0.71 yards (0.65 m)
- **Thread count:** 325 threads
- **Finished width after shrinking:** 0.63 yards (0.58 m)
- **Weave length:** 0.87 yards (0.80 m)
- **Warp length:** 1.31 yards (1.2 m)
- **Amount:** 0.44 oz (0.2 kg) felted wool and 1.75 oz (50 g) merino superwash

Threading, tie up, and treadle: Weave a plain weave (tabby) hem of roughly 1½ inches (4 cm) with the felted wool. Add the double knit merino in a plain weave; shed and pull the bobbles onto a knitting needle at regular intervals, about ½ inch (1.2 cm) apart. Add 3 felted wool wefts between every bobble round. End with a plain weave (tabby).

Wash the fabric and shrink it, then either felt it by hand or in the tumble dryer (see pages 107–108).

Fold the material double and place the pattern parts on it and cut them out. Use a zigzag seam around each part. Pin together the thumb parts (A) and the inside of the mittens, right sides together; the boucle will be on the wrong side. Sew together the top part of the mitten (1) with the inside of the mitten (2 a+b) right sides together, on a machine with an elastic seam. Finally crochet around all the seams with a color of your choice. Fold in the tabby edge at the bottom of the mitten and sew with a sewing machine. Fold up the bottom part so that the boucle creates a decorative edge and secure it in the side seams. Press the seams lightly using a steam iron.

Annelie's Mittens

Annelie finds sewing mittens very convenient, as you can use your own hand to try them on for size. She has made a pair from a sweater that has been felted. The pattern is made by needle felting and embroidery.

- **Skill level:** Average

Needle felting is done by placing carded wool on a felted base fabric of the required shape; this is then pinned into place with a special felting needle with little notches. The carded wool is then felted together with the base fabric.

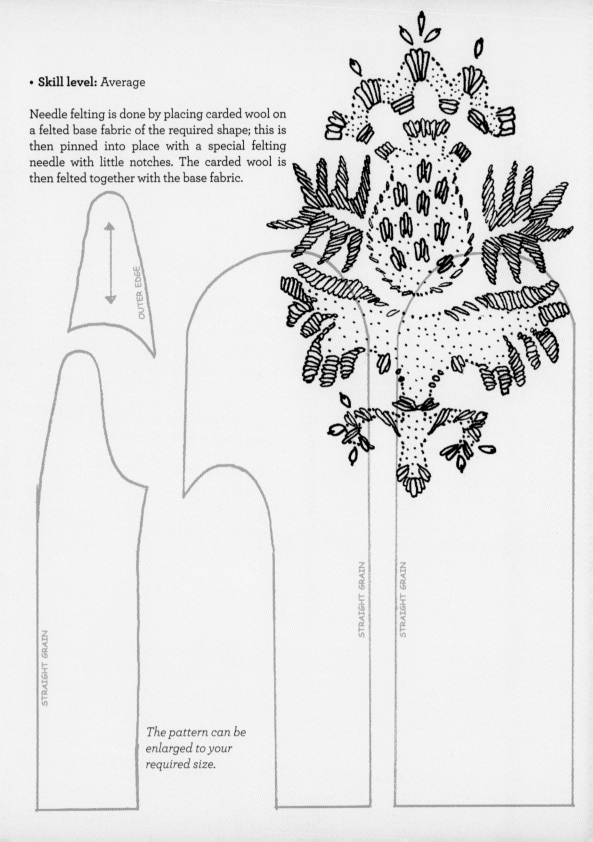

OUTER EDGE

STRAIGHT GRAIN

STRAIGHT GRAIN

STRAIGHT GRAIN

The pattern can be enlarged to your required size.

Karlsson's Winter Mittens

Kerstin A. has sewn a pair of mittens for her sweetheart. She recycled an old worn leather jacket with a fur lining, resulting in a pair of fancy mittens with detailing from the jacket (see page 15). It doesn't get warmer than this! Kerstin A. also contributed with the sewn white mittens that can be seen on page 58.

- **Skill level:** Average

The pattern can be enlarged to your required size.

Nalbinding Mittens

Nalbinding
—Every Busy Bee's Dream

Eva has worked as a handicrafts consultant nearly all her life, and one of her specialties is Nalbinding (also known as knotless knitting, knotless netting, and single needle knitting). This ancient technique has been used for hundreds of years to transform woolen yarn into warm and durable items of clothing—such as socks and mittens. Insoles were knotlessly knitted from tallow. This technique has been used all over the country, but it's mainly found in Mälardalen and around the Lake Mälar region, where the skills have been preserved. A few women scattered across Sweden have been fascinated by the technique, and they've made durable items of clothing with it. After a time, the craft became popular amongst a wider audience, and then a host of new ideas for clothes began to appear.

This technique is based on eyelets that are sewn into each other, making the clothes sparse, elastic, and easy to shape. Nalbinding is sewn with one needle in a sort of multiblanket stitch. It's made with short pieces of yarn; you felt a new piece of short yarn to another piece of short yarn by spitting at the ends and rubbing them until the yarn looks like one solid "thread."

The combination of the woolen yarn, the technique, and the felting, makes the clothes warm and practically indestructible. If a pair of mittens made in this manner get wet in the snow or rain, the fantastic properties of the wool will keep them feeling warm and cozy.

You can make your own patterns, and in this way you won't be dependent on the weight of the yarn or the tools to get a good product.

With regular knitting, the pattern, yarn, and needles are all dependent on each other to make the best result. As you use a needle to sew, the threads need to be joined together frequently. Just pull the yarn to break it—this will give you an uneven end. Moisten one end and place the two yarn ends around each other, and rub them together. In this way the joint is barely visible.

The tool used is a small needle about 2–4 inches (5–10 cm) long, made from metal, plastic, bone, antler, or wood. The work doesn't take up much space, which makes it handy, and in the same way as with knitting Nalbinding almost anywhere.

To learn the techniques of Nalbinding, we recommend looking for demonstrations on YouTube!

Socks

For the longest time I thought that socks always started at the cuff and ended at the toes. What a load of baloney! It doesn't have to be done like that at all. I was very surprised the first time I saw a pair of socks that were knitted starting at the toes and working upward. This is the way the last pair of socks in this book are made.

Baby Socks

In the 1950s, little girls were raised to be wives and mothers. This was also the idea behind home economics classes; we never made anything we could use ourselves, but instead learned how to make baby clothes. We were "preparing for adult life," so we weren't even allowed to make doll clothes. Sewing and knitting were "not for little boys." So I was really surprised to find out my father had knitted these for me when my mother was expecting.

- **Size:** Baby
- **Yarn:** Visjö from Östergötlands woolen mill, about 1600 yd/lb (3000 m/kg)
- **Amount:** 0.70 oz (20 g)
- **Needles:** Size 4 (3.5 mm)
- **Skill level:** Easy

The sock is knitted in garter stitch. Knit the last stitch on every round twisted and slip the first stitch to give you a nice edge. Cast on 12 stitches and knit a round. On the next round increase before the last 2 stitches by knitting the loop between 2 stitches twisted. Increase in this way at the end of each round until you have 24 stitches. Then decrease at the end of each round by knitting 2 stitches together inside the 2 outer stitches. When you have 12 stitches left, cast on 6 new stitches on one side, and on the other side increase at the end of each round until you have 24 stitches. Bind off 12 stitches on the side where you cast on 6 stitches and knit 12 rounds. Then cast on 12 stitches and decrease until 18 stitches remain. Sew the sock together; the straight part is crinkled against the tip of the sole. A placket is made from 5 stitches.

This sock is quite loosely knitted and has been lightly felted, meaning it's been hand washed in warm water with some soap. Keep working it until the felting process is complete.

It's easy to vary the size of the sock by changing needle size or the number of stitches. Look at the main pattern: You cast on an even number of stitches; the whole pattern will then be based on the fact that you increase and decrease, and cast on and bind off with the same amount, or half the amount, that you cast on.

1 square = 1 stitch and 2 rounds of garter stitch.

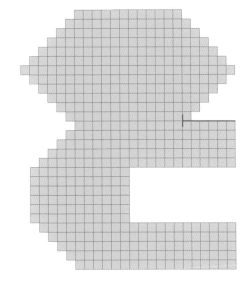

Winter Socks

These thick winter socks (known as ragg socks in Swedish) are made using three colors and are easy to knit. The heel is made last and, funnily enough, is made in the same way as the toe. A benefit of knitting the heel in this way is that it can easily be replaced if it gets torn or worn out.

- **Size:** About 7 years of age
- **Yarn:** The black sheep's yarn (Svarta Fårets raggsocksgarn) (70% wool, 30% synthetics, about 850 yd/lb [1600 m/kg]). A piece of cotton yarn is also required.
- **Amount:** 3 skeins of 1.75 oz (50 g) each in different colors
- **Needles:** Size 6 (4 mm). Two short circular needles, one long circular needle, and sock needles
- **Skill level:** Easy

Cast on 40 stitches and knit in rib stitch, 2 knit, 2 purl, for around 6 inches (16 cm). Knit two rows in stockinette stitch. Knit in a cotton thread over half the stitches and thread these stitches back on the needle, and then knit using the woolen yarn, changing color at the same time. The foot is made 4½ inches (11.5 cm) long. Change color and decrease at the toe. Half the stitches are the top side and half the stitches make the bottom. At the beginning and end of the top and bottom, knit 2 stitches together. Decrease by 4 stitches on each round. On one side, they are knitted together normally and on the other side twisted. When 8 stitches remain, remove the yarn and pull the thread through the stitches. Pull out the cotton thread, place the stitches on a needle and knit a similar "toe" for the heel.

Other sizes
You need to know what the gauge will be like with the yarn and needles you plan to use, so make a test patch. Measure around the front of the foot of the person who the sock is for and then calculate how many stitches you need, bearing in mind the sock should feel a bit tight! Cast on and knit. Keep testing and checking for when the rib and the foot section are long enough. Knit the toe and the heel.

The socks featured here have a simplified heel, known as a triangle heel.

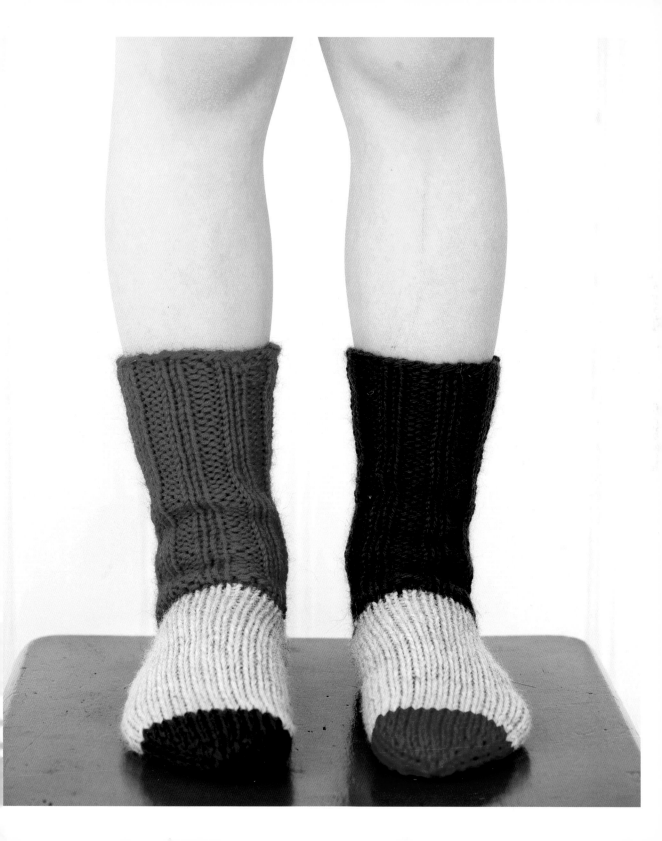

The Simplest Socks

These socks are so clever and really earn their name, as they are knitted in the form of a tube. The only difference is that you need to decrease so that the sock fits around the toes. Also, as they don't have heels, they don't wear out as quickly. They also fit lots of different sizes.

- **Size:** 7 years
- **Yarn:** The black sheep's yarn (Svarta Fårets Raggsocksgarn), (70% wool, 30% synthetics, about 850 yd/lb [1600 m/kg])
- **Amount:** 2 skeins of 1.75 oz (50 g)
- **Needles:** Two short circular needles, one long circular needle at least 23½ inches (60 cm) long, or sock needles size 6 (4 mm)
- **Skill level:** Easy

The socks are made with a number of stitches that can be divided by 4.

Cast on 40 stitches and knit in rib stitch, 2 knit and 2 purl, for 10 rounds. Then start the spiral knitting, displace the rib one stitch after 3 rounds (see picture). When the sock measures 12½ inches (32 cm), make the toe. Knit 1 round in stockinette stitch, then knit 2 stitches together 4 times, evenly distributed over every round until 8 stitches remain. As the sock doesn't have a topside or a sole, the toe doesn't need to be decreased so it lies flat.

Other sizes

For other sizes, calculate the number of stitches needed by measuring around the front of the foot and making a test patch. For larger sizes, you can make the spiral by knitting 4 or 5 rounds before you displace the ribbing.

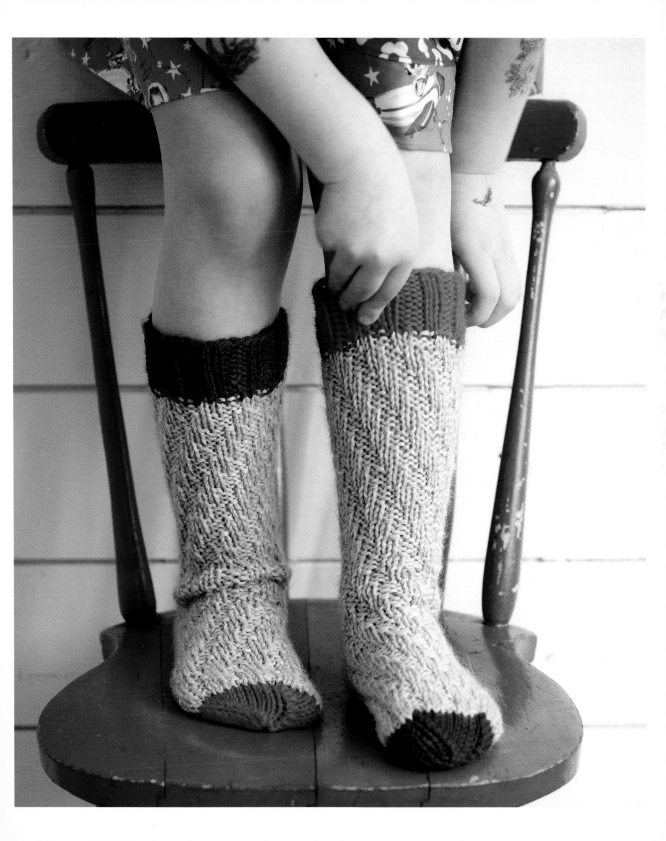

Socks with Legs

Many years ago, I came into contact with knitting from different cultures and eventually this led to a book. One of the women in the book was named Katarina. She who grew up in Estonia and moved to Sweden as a young newlywed. For the book, she knitted red sock legs that were kept in place with thick plaited bands and white socks like those she had worn as a young woman. I'll never forget her stories of how young women walked barefoot in the dewy grass with red leg warmers. I'll also always remember how Katarina used several pairs of leg warmers to fit in with what was considered beautiful at the time—to have thick shins. Here we revive the concept of a sock with a loose leg—just imagine how much easier it is to knit a new sock foot when the old one's worn out.

Leg

- **Size:** Smaller/larger
- **Yarn:** Visjö in several colors, 2-ply wool with about 1600 yd/lb (3000 m/kg) or remnants of similar quality
- **Amount:** 3½ oz (100 g)
- **Needles:** Size 1 (2.5 mm). Two short circular needles, one long circular needle, or sock needles
- **Gauge:** 16 stitches/2 inches (5 cm)
- **Skill level:** Easy

Cast on 68/72 stitches and knit in rib stitch, 1 knit, 1 purl, for about 1 inch (2 cm). Then create stripes by knitting 8 rounds in each color. Knit straight for about 4½ inches (11–12 cm) and then decrease 1 stitch on each side of the two middle stitches at the back of the leg on every 8th round. 1 stitch is decreased twisted and the other one decreased normally.

Decrease 8 times. When the leg measures roughly 13 inches (33/34 cm), knit 1 inch (2 cm) in rib stitch, 1 knit, 1 purl.

Bind off, secure the threads, and knit the second leg—and two socks.

You can weave the threads into your work when you change color to avoid securing them.

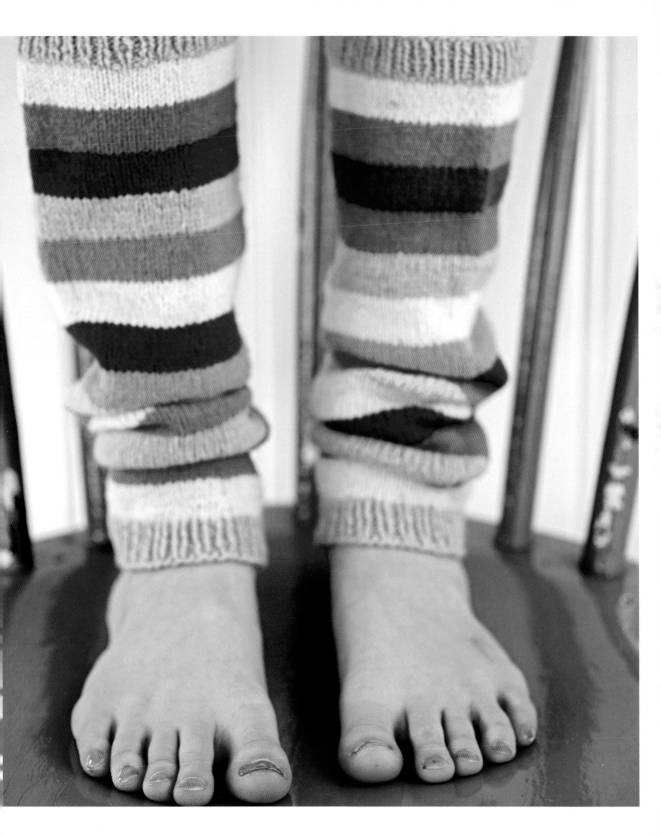

Socks

- **Yarn:** Visjö white from Östergötlands woolen mill, about 1600 yd/lb (3000 m/kg)
- **Amount:** About 3½ oz (100 g)
- **Needles:** Size 1 (2.5 mm). Two short circular needles, one long circular needle, or sock needles
- **Gauge:** 16 stitches/2 inches (5 cm)
- **Skill level:** Average

Cast on 54 stitches or according to the size of the front part of your foot, and knit in rib stitch, 1 knit, 1 purl, for 20 rounds. Then knit in stockinette stitch for 10 rounds.

The heel can be knitted in two ways:

First method

Knit on back and forth half the number of stitches. Knit shorter rounds (turn inside the outermost stitch, slip the first stitch, and knit to the end of the round), until a fifth of the stitches remain (here we have 5 stitches) and then knit extended rounds. To make the transition neatly, pick up a new stitch at the same time as you turn—this stitch gets knitted together with the outermost stitch—, slip a stitch and turn. When you have knitted all the stitches, continue round on the 54 stitches until you get to the toe. The toe area is knitted in the same way as the heel and is knitted on the stitches of the sole. When the toe area is finished, turn the knitting inside out and bind the stitches off together, one from the top side and one from the sole.

Second Method

When you come to knit the heel, place half the stitches on a thread. New stitches are picked up in the spaces between the stitches on the thread (make sure you get the right amount). Knit the foot. For the toe area, decrease on the sides by knitting 2 stitches together on each side inside the outermost stitch. One side is knitted twisted and the other is knitted normally. The decreasing takes place on every second round. When a fifth of the stitches on each side (here we have 5 stitches) remain, bind off and sew the stitches together. For the heel, take the stitches off the thread and knit them in the same way as the toe.

Pop Socks

Gisela weaves a lot and sometimes there are left over thrums (short fringes or remnants at the start and the end of the weave). This pattern for mittens and socks is especially useful for those who weave using woolen yarn in the warp; you can knit using remnants of pure wool. Woolen yarn does have a tendency to felt, which synthetic yarn does not.

- **Size:** Choose a pattern for socks/mittens and knit according to the largest size or make your own template to knit from
- **Yarn:** Woolen thrums or remnants in pure wool in various densities and yarn count
- **Needles:** Size 7 (4.5 mm) for the leg and size 8 (5 mm) for the stockinette stitch. Two short circular needles, one long circular needle or sock needles
- **Skill level:** Easy

Cast on in double yarn with long enough threads to cover all the stitches. Knit with one, alternatively two or three threads in a "string," depending on the thickness of the thrum. All threads in a "string" should be of varying lengths, and when there are roughly 3 inches (7 cm) left of a thread in the "string," take a new thrum thread and continue. The 3 inch (7 cm) bit and the new thread are knitted doubled up for about 4–5 stitches.

Let a bit of yarn of about 1 inch (2–3 cm) of the swapped thread hang down the back and carry on knitting until it's time to swap to the next thread.

When the knitting is complete, pull all the thread ends over to the wrong side of your work.

Felt in the washing machine: Place the socks with another load of washing in a 104°F (40°C) color wash. Stretch the socks after the wash. They should go through the machine two or three times and be stretched after every wash; it doesn't matter if they dry between washes. To see if the felting process is complete, grab the end of a thread and pull to see if the yarn moves on the right side of the piece. If it does, wash it once more. When the stitch doesn't move anymore the felting is complete and you can cut the threads on the inside of the sock.

Mittens can be made in the same way. Knit loosely with thick needles using several threads.

Glorious Socks
And Mittens

Last but not least we have two slightly more grandiose patterns:
Margareta's family socks and Kalli's fingerless mittens. They are slightly
more difficult to knit but once they are finished you will have something that
you can treasure for the rest of your life.

Kalli's Mittens

These mittens are not for beginners, but are rather a project for the avid knitter. Kalli was raised in Sweden but has her roots in Estonia. Her mother was an extraordinarily clever knitter and made thin, delicate white shawls with classic patterns. For this book Kalli has lent us a pair of fingerless mittens that reflect both history and beauty.

- **Size:** Ladies
- **Yarn:** Silla, 30% silk, 70% worsted yarn, about 2700 yd/lb (5000 m/kg)
- **Amount:** 1.75 oz (50 g) white, and some dark blue
- **Needles:** Size 000 or 4/0 (1.5 or 1.25 mm). Sock needles
- **Gauge:** 24 stitches/2 inches (5 cm)
- **Skill level:** Difficult

The mittens are made according to the diagram, which shows the number of stitches required. When you get to the fingers, try the mittens on to see where you need to make the divide for the fingers and cast on a few new stitches in the spaces.

1 row of knit stitches between
the rows of patterns

+ 3 st   + 3 st

104 st

96 st

94 st

© KALLI KLEMENT

	knit stitch
–	purl stitch
o	yarn over
⌒	2 together in knit stitch
ω	3 together in knit stitch
\	slip one stitch forwards, knit the next stitch, and then knit the slipped stitch in knit stitch
/	slip one stitch backwards, knit the next stitch in knit or purl stitch (depending on the pattern)
<	Slanted stitch: Place a stitch on a separate knitting needle, knit the next stitch and then the stitch that you placed on the separate needle. Place this new stitch onto the separate needle, and knit the next one, then the slipped stitch. This will give you a stitch that lies diagonal across the others.
■<	Same as < but with two colors.

Margareta's Family Socks

Margareta, who we've mentioned before, makes beautiful socks for her entire family. The socks have since become a family tradition. The patterns originate in Turkey and are knitted from the toe upward, which is often how socks are made in the East, in Turkey or Afghanistan, for example. I hope it will become a tradition for other families as well.

- **Size:** Ladies
- **Yarn:** Peer Gynt
- **Amount:** 3½ oz (100 g) dark and 3½ oz (100 g) light
- **Needles:** Size 2 needles and crochet hook C (3 mm)
- **Gauge:** 24 stitches stocking/4 inches (10 cm)
- **Skill level:** Difficult

Using a dark yarn and crochet hook C, cast on 10 stitches and with the yarn pick up 10 stitches along each side of the chain stitches and divide them across four needles = 5 stitches on each needle. These stitches create the stripes along the sides of the socks.

Increase: Pick up the thread between 2 stitches on the previous round, place it on the left needle and knit in knit stitch from behind.

Round 1: Knit the stitches on the 1st and 2nd needles with the dark yarn, increase 1 stitch with a light yarn between the 2nd and 3rd needles and place it on the 2nd needle—increase as per the pattern—knit the stitches on the 3rd and 4th needles with dark yarn and twine the light yarn with the dark and increase 1 stitch in light yarn between the 4th and 1st needles and place on the 4th needle.

Round 2: 1st needle and 3rd needle: 2 dark stitches, 1 light stitch, 2 dark stitches. 2nd and 4th needles: 2 dark stitches, 1 light stitch, 2 dark stitches, increase 1 light stitch, 1 dark stitch, increase 1 light stitch.

Round 3: 1st and 3rd needles: 1 dark stitch, 1 light stitch, 1 dark stitch, 1 light stitch, 1 dark stitch. 2nd and 4th needles: 1 dark stitch, 1 light stitch, 1 dark stitch, 1 light stitch, 1 dark stitch, increase 1 light stitch, 1 dark stitch, 1 light stitch, 1 dark stitch, increase 1 light stitch.

Round 4: 1st and 3rd needles: 2 dark stitches, 1 light stitch, 2 dark stitches. 2nd and 4th needles: 2 dark stitches, 1 light stitch, 2 dark stitches, increase 1 light stitch (1 dark stitch, 1 light stitch) twice, 1 dark stitch, increase 1 light stitch.

Round 5: 1st needle (1 dark stitch, 1 light stitch) twice, 1 dark stitch, knit the 2nd needle's first 5 stitches onto the 1st needle (1 dark stitch, 1 light stitch) twice, 1 dark stitch = the side section's 10 stitches. 2nd needle: Increase 1 gray stitch (1 dark stitch, 1 light stitch) three times, 1 dark stitch, increase 1 light stitch = the top part. 3rd needle: =1st needle but the first 5 stitches on the 4th needle are passed over to the 1st. 4th needle: = 2nd needle = the underside of the work.

Place a thread where the 1st needle begins. Continue to knit according to the pattern and increase as before on needles 2 and 4 until you have 21 stitches on needles 2 and 4. When you get to the heel on the pattern, place the 21 stitches on needle 4, and 5 stitches from each of needles 1 and 3 on a thread and as many stitches are cast on again. Keep knitting according to the pattern. When the pattern is complete, knit 3 rounds in light yarn and 3 rounds where every second stitch is light and every second dark, then 3 rounds in light yarn. Turn the work and knit x 1 round knit stitch from the wrong side, turn and knit 1 round knit stitch from the right side, repeat from x once more, turn and bind off with knit stitches from the wrong side. Pick up the stitches for the heels = the side section's 10 stitches, onto needles 1 and 3 and the heels under and over side onto needles 2 and 4. Knit 1 round and knit the patterns as usual on needles 1 and 3 and on the other needles knit the pattern according to the diagram. Knit 2 knit stitches together on every round on each side on needles 2 and 4. When only the side section's 10 stitches remain, bind off these stitches and sew them together.

Sew the hem at the top of the sock.

Tips and Hints

Terms Used

Garter stitch: All the rows are in knit stitch when you knit back and forth. If you want an edge that looks like garter stitch when you are knitting with circular needles, every one round is in knit and every other round is in purl.

Stockinette stitch: If you are knitting in a round, all the stitches are in knit stitch. If you are knitting back and forth on a row, alternate between knit and purl.

Binding off: When binding off, divide the stitches over two needles, one stitch is taken from each needle and treated as one stitch. Bind off as usual.

Make a Test Patch

If you have yarn and needles and want to knit, but you're not sure which pattern to use, you can benefit from making a test patch. Cast on 26 stitches for a heavier yarn and 36 for a lighter one. Knit a few rounds in garter stitch and then move to stockinette stitch, making sure you knit the 3 outermost stitches on each side in knit stitch for all rows. Finish off with a few rows of garter stitch and make sure your patch is equal all around. If you plan to knit using a pattern, you need to make your patch with a pattern, and if the pattern is in several colors, it's easiest to knit in a round. Knitting with several colors and knitting in stockinette stitch with one color does not give the same gauge. Even when crocheting, it is worth making a test patch. If you are unsure of which crochet hook or knitting needle to use, you can try several different ones just by knitting or crocheting a few rows using the different tools. Carefully note which yarn you used or leave a bit of yarn hanging so you have something to compare with later. Wash the test patch.

This may sound ambitious, but I can guarantee that you will appreciate your test patches, as they will become a collection of quality tests. The same yarn has to be knitted or crocheted with different gauges depending on what you're making. Socks and mittens need to be knitted fairly tightly, whereas a scarf or sweater that is softer needs to be made looser.

Knitting with Several Colors

It's a lot easier to knit in a round with several colors than knitting a row. A few technical pointers would probably be useful right now:
- Try finding a pattern where the threads don't need to run behind the work for more than 3 stitches.
- It's always best to let the yarns lie in the same way on the index finger throughout the knitting, one over the other.
- If the threads run behind for 4, 5, or more stitches, you need to "weave in" the thread you are not knitting with. You do this by placing the thread you are knitting with under the running thread and at the next stitch, over the running thread.
- Knit so that the running threads don't pull the knitting together.
- Don't forget that when you knit with several colors, the gauge will be different than when you knit with one color.

Yarn

Picking the yarn depends on what you're making. A yarn with some synthetic fibers can be durable when making children's mittens or socks that need to wear well, and it's often cheaper than pure wool. However, if you're looking for warmth, you need the highest percentage to be wool.

Kitchener Stitch

It can sometimes be tricky when you want to knit a pattern that is just the one figure. However, there is another option and this is to embroider the image using kitchener stitch. It's easy and the result is just as elastic as the rest of the knitting.

Kitchener stitch that follows the round widthwise will look great stitch after stitch. If you want to embroider height-wise, it's sometimes easier to get the stitches looking neat if you sew in two rounds, first do every second stitch and then go back and do the skipped ones. Put one of your hands inside the mitten or a piece of paper inside it so that you don't sew the front and back together.

Two at a Time

It's always a good idea to knit right and left mittens or socks at the same time, and this means that you need double the equipment when it comes to needles and yarn. Alternate the knitting between the left and right mitten, as this makes it easier to get them to match. I personally find it quite satisfying to finish them both at the same time.

However, as I'm writing this, I realize that there is no reason why they should look like each other. They can look different and still belong to each other.

Different Ways of Knitting a Round

Personally I think knitting with a long circular needle is the quickest way and I get a better result than when knitting on four needles. This is how you do it: use a circular needle that's at least 23½ inches (60 cm) long. The number of stitches are divided by two and these are the stitches that you knit with. In order for it to work, you pull out the "tube" that connects the needles between the middle stitches. In this way you can knit sleeves and hats in a round instead of knitting them flat and then sewing them together.

To knit using two shorter circular needles is another way to avoid having five straight sock needles to keep track of.

Increasing and Decreasing

Increase: Between the stitches on the previous round there's a loop, pick it up on the left needle and knit it twisted.

Decrease: If you want a left leaning decrease, knit two stitches together twisted. If you want a right leaning decrease, knit two stitches together. When you decrease at the fingertips or toes, the right decrease should lean to the left and the left lean to the right. Sound confusing? It's easier than it sounds.

Finishing Off

When the mitten or sock is finished, you will have seams to sew, threads to secure, and the item will need to be washed or soaked. All the clothes in this book are made from woolen yarns, although the socks might have a small mix of synthetic in them to make them last longer. Wash by hand in lukewarm water and use some washing detergent for wool or a shampoo, as woolen yarn is made from sheep's hair. Lay the items out to dry and shape them while they are damp. Wet items that are hung up can stretch lengthwise and lose their shape. When they have dried you can see how fantastic they look. Washing them is really the icing on the cake, as all the stitches settle down and that which looked half-perfect before, now looks completely perfect.

Felting

Mittens and socks can be treated so that the woolen yarn felts. After you have felted it, the clothing will be soft and the stitches and threads become fixed. However, a word of caution: Be careful and do a sample before you felt a completed project, as some people have ended up with something quite small and hard when the process has been too dramatic.

Felting items of clothing will cause them to shrink, so in order for them to become beautifully felted they need to be knitted loosely. Felted items end up warm and dense and felted socks are much more durable than nonfelted ones.

If you want complete control of the felting process, felt your clothes by hand. This means preparing warm water with either soap or olive soap and then rubbing the clothing or weave against a washboard. It can be hard work, but it's very controlled and you can shape the item during the process. This is the way in which you treat Nalbinding items.

You can also felt woolen items in the washing machine. It's important to know that woolen fibers are heat resistant. It might seem strange when the label says to wash in lukewarm water, but you can actually use quite a high heat. What affects the felting is the mechanical process. Let the clothes soak for quite a while before placing them in the washing machine.

Place the item in the washing machine and, as all machines are different, we are not giving you exact directions here. Get the machine going and if you are happy with the results then that's great. If not? Well, just redo the process, but not with warmer water or a different program; just do exactly the same thing until you are happy with the result.

A third way to felt is to soak the items you want to treat and run them through the tumble dryer. This also makes it easy to control the result, as you can stop the drying cycle and see how things are proceeding.

So as you can see, felting can be tricky but it's also fun. The results you get when a coarse item of clothing becomes soft and touchable is a source of joy, but be sure to make a note of how you've done it, as it's easy to forget.

Further Reading

Our first tip is to go to the library! Check out secondhand book shops, scour thrift stores, borrow books from your mother or grandmother, and search the Internet. Here are just a few tips for further reading:

- Christoffersson, Britt-Marie, *Swedish Sweaters: New Designs from Historical Examples,* 1990
- Dandanell, Birgitta, *Twined Knitting: A Swedish Folkcraft Technique.* 1989.
- Lind, Vibeke, *Knitting in the Nordic Tradition.* 1997.
- *Nilsson, Ann-Mari, Quick Nordic Knits: 50 Socks, Hats and Mittens.* 2010.
- Pagoldh, *Susanne, Nordic Knitting: Thirty-one patterns in the Scandinavian Tradition.* 1992.
- Righetti, Maggie, *Knitting in Plain English.* 2007.
- Anderson, Eva, *Nålbindning. Historiskt och modernt i Stockholms län.* Stockholm 2009

Some Blogs

- *The Yarn Harlot* www.yarnharlot.ca/blog
- *The Panopticon* the-panopticon.blogspot.com/
- *Ysolda* www.ysolda.com/blog/
- *My Sister's Knitter* mysistersknitter.typepad.com/my-blog/
- *Twist Collective* www.twistcollective.com/collection/blog

Yarn

Herrviks Farm

is a small family company run by Johan and Kerstin. They produce wool for one and two-ply ecological yarns in natural colors. By mixing wool from lambs and sheep they create a soft yarn. They also make a yarn made from flax and wool. The wool comes from sheep that are crossbred,, mainly fine wool, Swedish fur, Leicester, and Texel sheep. Kerstin is interested in wool. The crossbreeding is carefully controlled, and she evaluates the results. The spinning takes place at various woolen mills. **www.herrvik.se**

Grimslätt Farm

is run by Sara and Marcus. Here they raise sheep from Gotland. During the summer the sheep graze on the broads in Fjällbacka's archipelago and Tjurpannan's nature reserve outside Grebbestad. The sun, salt, and mineral rich pasture produce a soft and shiny wool, and during the winter the sheep are kept on the farm where they roam freely. The sheep's fleece and wool have a unique combination of soft and warm underwool and strong and shiny guard hairs, making the wool both waterproof and durable. **www.grimslatt.se**

Östergötlands Woolen Mill

is situated in Storeryd and makes yarn using traditional methods. Production and processing takes place in the factory using the old ways. The wool is picked with care and is spun on a Spinning Jenny, a machine that originates from the eighteenth century. The company is run by Ulla-Karin and Börje Hellsten. **www.ullspinneriet.com**

Ullcentrum on Öland

was started at the end of the 1990s by Ann Linderhjelm. One of the reasons they collect and spin locally produced wool is that, sadly, a lot of Swedish wool gets burned. Ullcentrum takes care of wool from Öland and the surrounding areas. **www.ullcentrum.com**

Kampes Spinning Products

makes yarn in Ullervad. The wool is mainly imported from New Zealand. **www.kampes.se**

Järbo Yarn

can be found in Gästrikland. Their yarns are sold in many different stores and Järbo also imports a lot of yarns. **www.jarbo.se**

A website I've found useful for ordering Swedish wool is: **www.swedishyarn.com**

Contributors to
*Warm Mittens
and Socks*

Eva Anderson
Kerstin Askert
Hedvig Elmlund
Mariana Eriksson
Björn Gavelin
Annelie Holmberg
Kalli Klément
Inger Klockar
Margareta Littmarck
Kerstin Lovallius
Kerstin Mörner
Mona Nordin
Kerstin Slåneteg
Annika Stier
Eva Torstenson
Gisela von Weisz
Erika Åberg